HEARTS OF GOLD

Reflections of

CREATIVE VOICE

Gold Award Girl Scouts

Sheryl M Robinson

Copyright Page

No part of this publication may be reproduced, stored in a retrieval system, or transmitted in any form or by any means — electronic, mechanical, photocopying, recording, or otherwise — without prior written permission from the author.

This book contains stories based on interviews with **Gold Award Girl Scouts**. "Girl Scout," "Girl Scouts," and "Gold Award" are registered trademarks of **Girl Scouts of the USA**, used in alignment with trademark guidelines for describing Girl Scouts.

Published by Grow and Share Network, LLC
First Edition, 2026

ISBN: 978-1-972135-03-7

Printed in the United States of America

Books in the Hearts of Gold Series

- *Earth Guardian*
- *STEM*
- *Creative Voice*
- *Health*
- *Inclusion*
- *Advocacy*
- *Community Connector*

Table of Contents

CHAPTER 1 —When Voices Speak
CHAPTER 2 — The CEO of Tomorrow
CHAPTER 3 — Success Closet
CHAPTER 4 — Preserving the Unspoken
CHAPTER 5 — Behind The Lens
CHAPTER 6 — The Voices of Silver Stories
CHAPTER 7 — Uncovering Miss Kitty's Secret
CHAPTER 8 — Map The County's Local Harvest
CHAPTER 9 — Reporting for Change
CHAPTER 10 — Hidden History
CHAPTER 11 —The Power Of The Silent Word
CHAPTER 12 —Life-Saving Choices
CHAPTER 13 —Your voice For Good

Acknowledgements
About the Author
Explore More Hearts of Gold Stories

Chapter 1
When Voices Speak

Noticing What's Unsaid

If you look around your school, your community, or even your own family, you might notice things that feel unfinished. A story no one talks about. A moment in history that's mentioned quickly and then skipped. A group of people who seem invisible, even though they're right there.

To a Creative Voice, these moments aren't accidents.

They're signals.

There are clues that something important is waiting to be noticed.

Across the country, girls just like you are paying attention to those clues. In this book, you'll meet girls who used creativity — writing, filmmaking, photography, art, interviews, design, podcasts, and storytelling — to shine light on what others overlooked. Their stories prove something powerful:

You don't have to be loud to be heard. You just need to be willing to begin.

Creative Voices don't always start with confidence. Many begin with curiosity. With questions that won't go away. With moments that feel confusing, unfair, or unfinished. Instead of ignoring those feelings, these girls leaned in.

And that made all the difference.

Telling Stories That Matter

Some Creative Voices focus on stories that have been ignored, misunderstood, or forgotten.

You'll meet girls who noticed that textbooks left out entire chapters of history — so they created new ways to teach them. Girls who realized that elders in their community held incredible memories — and found ways to preserve their voices before they were lost. Girls who understood that when stories disappear, understanding disappears with them.

These projects didn't start with cameras or microphones.

They started with listening.

Listening to family members. Listening to neighbors. Listening to silence.

Each of these girls noticed a gap and asked themselves a brave question: "What happens if no one tells this story?"

Instead of waiting for someone else to act, they stepped forward.

They researched. They interviewed. They wrote, recorded, filmed, and designed with care. They learned that telling someone else's story comes with responsibility — and that respect matters just as much as creativity.

Through their work, they helped communities remember, learn, and heal.

Creativity as a Tool for Change
🎬 🎬 🎬 🎬 🎬

Other Creative Voices noticed something different.

They saw confusion. Stigma. Misinformation. Topics people avoided because they felt uncomfortable or complicated. Instead of staying silent, these girls used creativity to start conversations.

You'll read about girls who used film, writing, and discussion to help others understand complex issues. Girls who built programs that taught younger kids how to tell their own stories. Girls who designed safe spaces for learning, reflection, and growth.

Their creativity wasn't about performance.

It was about connection.

They learned that art and media can explain what facts alone sometimes cannot. Those stories can build empathy. That, when people see themselves reflected, they feel less alone.

These projects required courage. Talking about real issues meant facing real emotions — their own and others'. Along the way, these girls learned how to communicate thoughtfully, accept feedback, and keep going even when the work felt heavy.

They discovered that creativity has power — especially when it's used with purpose.

What Makes a Creative Voice Different?

Creative Voices share a few important strengths.

First, they notice what's missing.

They pay attention to whose stories aren't being told and whose voices aren't being heard. They don't assume silence means something doesn't matter.

Second, they learn before they create.

They ask questions. They research. They talk to experts and listen to people with lived experience. They understand that good storytelling starts with understanding.

Third, they believe stories can change people.

Because they can.

Creative Voices don't wait to feel like experts. They grow into leadership by doing the work — learning new skills, fixing mistakes, and trying again.

Being a Creative Voice isn't about being perfect or artistic in one specific way. It's about caring enough to speak up when something important feels unfinished.

Your Voice Belongs Here Too

As you read the chapters ahead, you'll meet girls who didn't always think of themselves as leaders, artists, or storytellers.

They were students. Readers. Athletes. Performers. Observers.

Some were quiet. Some were busy. Some were unsure if their ideas mattered.

What they shared was a choice.

They chose not to ignore the questions that stayed with them.

They chose to learn.   They chose to try.

And through that process, they discovered something important: leadership doesn't always look like standing at the front of a room. Sometimes it looks like holding a microphone for someone else. Sometimes it looks like writing late at night. Sometimes it looks like editing, revising, and starting over.

Maybe your passion is history.
Maybe it's art, film, writing, music, or design.
Maybe it's helping others feel understood.
Maybe it's noticing a story that feels unfinished.
Whatever keeps pulling at your attention — that's
        where your journey begins.

This book is full of courage, creativity, and real examples from girls who spoke up when it mattered.

The world needs storytellers.   Your voice is one of them.

Chapter 2
The CEO of Tomorrow

Rachel Holmes (Ep 73)

The Spark Of Innovation

Rachel Holmes was never the type of student who just sat back and watched things happen; she was a girl with a plan and the drive to see it through. Long before she began her project, she was already a seasoned Girl Scout, having been a member since kindergarten. In middle school, Rachel teamed up with her sister, Briana, to create "Art Cart," a project where they stocked a cart with art supplies and coloring books and delivered it to their local children's hospital to provide a creative escape for young patients. This history of helping others was the foundation upon which she would build her most ambitious project yet.

In high school, Rachel found her stride in business and entrepreneurship. She wasn't just taking classes; she was competing in high-stakes challenges like the World Series of Innovation and a districtwide Career and Technical Education (CTE) innovation challenge. At the CTE competition, Rachel's brilliance shone through when she took home first place for an idea she called "Funds for Females". The concept was simple yet powerful: providing grants to women entrepreneurs to help them turn their dreams into reality. This victory was more than just a trophy on a shelf; it was the spark that ignited a bigger vision. Rachel realized that while money was necessary, mentorship and skill-building were the real keys to long-term success for women in business.

When it came time to select her project, Rachel's mind went straight back to her passion for business. Initially, she considered creating a general website to connect business professionals with students from all backgrounds. However, after talking with her mother, who suggested a focus on mentoring, Rachel began to reflect on her own identity and her road ahead. As a young Black woman, Rachel knew that she would face unique obstacles in the corporate world. She realized that Black women often navigate the problematic intersection of "both sexism and racism in the workplace". She decided that her project needed to be more "tangible and more personal," and thus, "Black Girls Mean Business" was born. Her mission was to create a specialized safe space for Black high school girls across the United States to develop their professional skills and gain the confidence to lead.

Designing The Blueprint

Rachel knew that an idea as big as "Black Girls Mean Business" needed a solid structure to be effective. She envisioned a virtual summer program that would act as a bridge between high school and the professional world. To make this a reality, she designed her curriculum around four essential pillars: mentoring from experienced professionals, workshops that inspired and taught fundamental skills, access to professional resources, and networking opportunities. Rachel wanted her participants to walk away not just with knowledge, but with a network of people who could help them throughout their careers. This required her to step into the role of a recruiter, reaching out to people far beyond her own circle of friends and family.

Building a team of mentors was one of the most critical steps in Rachel's execution plan. She didn't want just anyone; she wanted established business people who could provide real-world insights. To find them, Rachel used several strategic methods to build her network:

Professional Partnerships: She worked closely with SCORE, a nonprofit organization that helps small businesses, to find and promote her program to their network of professionals.

Social Media Leveraging: Rachel's father shared the program on his LinkedIn account, opening doors to a vast network of business leaders eager to volunteer.

Cold Email Outreach: She spent hours researching local and national businesses, sending professional emails to see if their employees would be interested in participating.

Digital Branding: Using Canva, Rachel designed a "beautiful" and professional Instagram account for the program, which became a primary tool for attracting both students and guest speakers.

Rachel found the feedback on Instagram "incredible," and the community's support gave her the momentum she needed. While she initially designed all the posts herself, the project eventually grew so much that she brought on volunteers to help manage the digital side. She learned that a successful leader knows how to delegate tasks and build a community around a shared goal. By creating a professional image for "Black Girls Mean Business," she proved that even a high school student could run an organization that professionals took seriously. Rachel was no longer just a student; she was the founder of a movement that was gaining national attention.

The Pandemic Pivot

As Rachel was finalizing her plans in early 2020, the world suddenly changed. Like many people at the time, Rachel "naively assumed that the pandemic would be over by the summer". She had spent months planning an in-person event at her school or a local business, but didn't have a backup plan for a virtual format. However, by the time she realized the COVID-19 pandemic wasn't going away, she had to choose: give up or adapt. Rachel chose to "quickly shift gears". She decided to move the entire program online, using Zoom for workshops and email for one-on-one mentoring.

Initially, the shift to virtual felt like a setback, but Rachel soon realized it was a "blessing in disguise". Because the program was no longer tied to a physical location, she could expand her reach far "outside of the Bay Area". Suddenly, she wasn't just helping girls in her own neighborhood; she was connecting with Black high school girls from across the United States. The virtual format also made it much easier to book high-level speakers who might not have had time to drive to an in-person event but were happy to hop on a Zoom call for an hour. Rachel's project was no longer a local summer camp; it had become a national resource.

Even with the new virtual plan, Rachel had to learn how to "think on her feet quite a bit". She faced unexpected challenges when mentors or speakers had to drop out at the last minute due to personal reasons. This could have derailed a lesser project, but Rachel stayed calm and worked to find substitutes. She was amazed to see that the mentors who stepped in at the last minute were "more than what I had imagined". This taught her a valuable lesson about leadership: things will rarely go exactly according to plan, but if you stay flexible and focused on your goal, the outcome can be even better than you originally hoped. Rachel transitioned from being a girl who followed a plan to a leader who could navigate a crisis with confidence.

Inside The Boardroom

🎤🎤🎤🎤🎤

The heart of "Black Girls Mean Business" was the series of workshops that Rachel carefully curated for her participants. She didn't want the sessions to feel like another boring school lecture; she wanted them to be interactive and immediately useful. One of the most popular and valuable sessions was the "interviews and applying to jobs" workshop led by Amanda. Amanda walked the girls through the modern job market, teaching them how to build professional LinkedIn profiles, write effective resumes, and navigate job applications. Rachel knew these were the skills that would give her participants an edge in a competitive world.

The highlight of that workshop was the mock Zoom interviews. Rachel organized breakout rooms where the girls could practice their interviewing skills with their mentors in real time. The participants loved the hands-on experience, and many reported that it was the most helpful part of the entire summer. Rachel also hosted a college workshop explicitly focused on the University of California (UC) schools. This session felt incredibly personal to Rachel because she was "working on my college applications and so were a lot of the other girls" at the same time. They weren't just learning from a teacher; they were a group of peers navigating a life milestone together.

Seeing the girls grow in confidence was the most rewarding part of the project for Rachel. She watched as they came to the sessions with nervous questions and left with clear goals and new skills. The feedback she received from the schools and participants was overwhelmingly positive, proving a massive need for this kind of support. Rachel realized that by sharing her own journey and creating this platform, she was helping other girls see that their voices mattered in the business world. She was providing the tools, but the girls were providing the ambition. For Rachel, this was a full-circle moment where her passion for business met her commitment to her community, creating a lasting impact that would help these future leaders for years to come.

A Mission Without End

Completing her project taught Rachel that being a leader is about much more than just a single project; it's about persistence and long-term vision. One of the biggest surprises for her was the sheer amount of work required for the "initial report as well as the final report". She realized that the paperwork involved was far more detailed than anything she had done in school. Her advice to future candidates is to "start as soon as possible" and to be "as specific as possible" in the project proposal. She learned that by accounting for every detail and asking for help from mentors and family, you can avoid the "loops of feedback" that often slow the process down.

Leadership growth was the most significant outcome for Rachel. She went from competing in school challenges to running a national virtual program with dozens of volunteers and participants. Even as she prepared to graduate high school and move on to a four-year university, Rachel knew she wasn't finished with "Black Girls Mean Business". She is working on the future program and adding more workshops and content to the curriculum. Her ultimate dream is to turn the program into an "official nonprofit" (501c3) with its own headquarters and the funding to provide even more resources, like an official Zoom account, to the girls who need them.

Rachel's life outside of her business mission is just as active and disciplined. She is an accomplished artistic swimmer who has competed for years with the Santa Clara Aquamaids, traveling and competing on a high level. Whether she is in the pool or in a virtual boardroom, Rachel carries the same level of focus and dedication. She has proven that age is not a barrier to making a difference and that a single girl can create a legacy that spans the entire country. As Rachel looks toward her college years and beyond, she remains committed to her role as a mentor and an advocate for the next generation of Black business leaders.

Rachel's journey shows us that her work is not about reaching a finish line, but about building a launchpad. Just as a seed needs the right soil and care to grow into a tall tree, Rachel provided the "mentorship soil" that allowed hundreds of young dreams to take root, ensuring that the future of business looks a lot more like the diverse world we live in.

Chapter 3
Success Closet

Jasmine Bartell (Ep 28)

The Heart Behind the Fashion

Jasmine Bartell always believed that a person's outfit could change how they felt about the world. For nearly nine years, she had been a Girl Scout learning about leadership and community service. She had spent seasons selling cookies at booths and nights telling stories around a campfire with her friends. She even remembered a special trip to Savannah, Georgia, where she visited the original headquarters and learned about the long history of girls making a difference. However, as she entered the final years of high school, she wanted to do something that genuinely reflected her personal passions. She didn't want just to follow a group; she wanted to lead a movement.

Her earlier work had been very different. In middle school, she worked with a group to create an alternative bike trail along the Silver Comet Trail in Hiram, Georgia. That project taught her about hard work and teamwork, but because it was a group effort, she didn't feel it fully reflected her own strengths. She realized that while building trails was helpful, her heart was really in fashion and advocacy for women. She wanted to combine her love of style with a desire to empower women going through the most challenging times of their lives.

Jasmine began researching different populations in her community who needed support. She discovered that many women who were survivors of domestic violence or who were living on low incomes struggled to find the resources they needed to start over. One of the biggest hurdles these women faced was finding appropriate clothes for job interviews. Without proper business attire, it was nearly impossible for them to retain employment and achieve independence. This struck a chord with Jasmine, and she decided her final project would be called "The Journey to Success".

Her initiative was clear: she would design a professional closet space right inside her high school. This wouldn't just be a place for old clothes; it would be a boutique-style environment where women could find beautiful business outfits and the resources they needed to feel confident and strong. Jasmine knew that helping a woman feel beautiful was the first step toward becoming the strong person she was meant to be. She wanted to give these women a "step closer to success" by providing the tools for a fresh start.

Assembling the Dream Team

Jasmine knew that a project of this size could not be done alone. To turn a space at Hiram High School into a professional clothing boutique, she needed to build a team of experts and supporters. In May 2018, she began reaching out to people who could help her navigate the complicated worlds of school administration and nonprofit work. She reached out to her principal, Cooksey Misty, to discuss using school space, and Kathryn Melton, the executive director of Shepherd's Rest Ministries. This ministry was a perfect partner because they already provided shelter for victims of domestic violence in the Paulding County area.

Connecting with these leaders required Jasmine to step out of her comfort zone. She had to explain her vision clearly and demonstrate a step-by-step plan to solve the problem. She also worked closely with her advisor, Nora Years, and her local leader, Paula Mensah, who helped her stay organized. Through these partnerships, Jasmine learned that being a leader isn't just about giving orders; it's about finding the right people who share your passion and giving them a reason to help you succeed.

Her team also included her peers and members of her community. She realized that to fill a closet, she would need more than a few donations; she would need a massive influx of professional clothing. She spent hours coordinating with different organizations and informing them about her goal. She discovered that when you create something meaningful, people are often surprisingly eager to jump in and help. Jasmine had to manage all these moving parts while also focusing on her schoolwork and future college plans.

This phase of the project taught Jasmine about the "human" side of leadership. She had to learn how to communicate with people from different backgrounds—from high school principals to directors of local ministries. She had to be persistent, sending emails, making phone calls, and attending meetings to ensure everyone was on the same page. She found that having a supportive group behind her was the only way to keep the project moving when things got difficult. By the time planning was finished, Jasmine had built a network of support as strong as the vision in her head.

From Vision to Reality

Once the plans were approved, the real physical labor began. Jasmine didn't just want to hang clothes on a rack; she wanted the space to feel like a high-end store. This required her to pick up tools she had never used before. She learned how to design a room layout and even how to apply paint to the walls. She decided to create an accent wall with different colors to make the room pop and feel welcoming. Every stroke of the brush was a lesson in patience and precision.

The execution of the project required Jasmine to develop a detailed, step-by-step solution to the problem. She had to focus on the logistics of the clothing drive, the interior design, and the marketing for the grand opening. To make sure the community knew about "The Journey to Success," she took the following actions:

Flyer Creation: She designed and printed over 100 flyers to inform the community about her mission and the specific types of professional clothing needed.

Donation Coordination: She set up a system to collect and sort through 384 items, ensuring every piece of clothing was appropriate and in good condition for job seekers.

Grand Opening Planning: She organized a formal event for August 18, 2018, to reveal the closet and celebrate the partnership with Shepherd's Rest Ministries.

Jasmine found that the actual building process was one of her most significant learning experiences. She discovered that she could look at a problem—like a dull, empty room—and develop a creative solution. Designing the closet wasn't just about where the racks went; it was about creating a positive atmosphere. She wanted the women who entered the closet to feel like they were entering a new chapter of their lives.

By the time the closet was finished, it was a phenomenal success. Jasmine had collected nearly 400 items through her outreach efforts. She had transformed a simple high school space into a

center of empowerment. The project had allowed
her to grow in ways she never expected, showing
her that she could do amazing things if she stayed
focused and didn't give up. The physical work of
painting and organizing was hard, but seeing the
result made every hour of labor worth it.

Impact and Recognition

The impact of the clothing closet was felt almost
immediately. By providing impoverished women
and survivors of domestic violence with appropriate
business attire and resources, Jasmine was
helping them break the cycle of poverty. Her
project ensured that a lack of professional clothing
would never be the reason a woman didn't get a
job. The result allowed these women to walk into
interviews with their heads held high, knowing they
looked the part.

The community's response was overwhelming.
Jasmine was invited to present her project to the
Paulding County Board of Commissioners.
Standing before the local government leaders was
a huge achievement and a moment of great pride
for her. They were impressed by her dedication
and the way she had identified a specific need and
solved it. This experience gave Jasmine the
confidence to speak up for what she believed in,
even in front of important officials.

Sustainability is a key part of any big project, and Jasmine made sure hers would last. She arranged for the clothing closet to be managed and sustained by the National Honor Society, a club she was active in during high school. Years after her project was completed, she heard back from the club that the closet was still doing "phenomenal" work in the community. Knowing that her hard work continued to help people even after she graduated was the greatest reward she could ask for.

Jasmine's favorite memory from the entire journey was the grand opening. Seeing all the pieces fall into place—the 384 items she had collected, the brightly painted accent wall, and the people from different organizations coming together—made her feel incredibly proud. She realized that her outreach had truly moved the community. The project changed how people viewed high school students; they saw that a girl could take an idea from scratch and turn it into a lasting institution that helped dozens of families.

Future Runways and Final Lessons

Jasmine's work on her project didn't just help her community; it also shaped her future. The experience of running a clothing closet and managing a team led her to realize she wanted to be an entrepreneur. She enrolled at the University of West Georgia to major in business management. Her dream job is to become a fashion consultant, where she can continue helping people style themselves and build the confidence to succeed in their careers. She wants to own her own business and work with various companies to promote positivity and empower women.

Looking back on her time in Girl Scouts, Jasmine values the skills she gained in communication and sales. She credits her time working at cookie booths with helping her become a great salesperson, a skill she used when she had to "sell" the idea of her clothing closet to donors and officials. She learned that whether she was selling a box of cookies or a vision for a better community, the key was to be passionate and never to give up, even when things got difficult.

Her advice to other girls who are starting their own projects is to choose something they truly love. "If you do a project that you hate doing and you're not even passionate about, why even do it?" she asked. She encourages others to pick a topic that makes them feel "carefree" and excited, because that passion is what will get them through the moments when they feel frustrated or defeated. Jasmine's journey taught her that she was not just a student; she was a leader capable of making a global impact through local action.

Jasmine Bartell's story shows that when you weave together passion and hard work, you can create a safety net for those who are falling. Her clothing closet stands as a symbol of hope, proving that a single girl's vision can dress a community in confidence and prepare them for the journey to success.

Chapter 4
Preserving the Unspoken

Erica Dunne (Ep 52)

Cookie Trail To History

Erica Dunne's journey into the heart of history began with a simple box of cookies and a knock on a door. Since she was only five years old, she had spent every Veterans Day traveling through her community with her troop to deliver treats to local heroes. As a young girl, she noticed a recurring and touching sight: the veterans were often already waiting by their doors, eager for the arrival of the local youth. When she and her friends stepped inside, they weren't just handing over snacks; they were stepping into living museums of bravery. These men and women would pull out old, dusty newspaper clippings and shiny service badges that they had kept for decades. They would share vivid stories of their time in the service, recounting moments of fear, friendship, and sacrifice that had shaped their lives.

The more Erica listened, the more she realized that these incredible accounts were at risk of being lost forever. Many veterans admitted that, apart from their closest family members, almost no one had ever asked them about their service. This realization struck a chord with Erica, sparking a deep personal motivation to document these voices. She didn't want these memories to fade away with the passage of time; she wanted to transform them into a permanent community resource. This wasn't just about history books found in a library; it was about the hidden stories of the people living right next door.

As she entered high school, Erica's passion for service and storytelling combined into a clear vision for her project. She knew she wanted to capture these veteran stories in a way that was both accessible and deeply respectful. Her goal was to bridge the gap between generations, helping her peers and younger children understand the true meaning of service. She believed that by documenting these experiences, she could create an everlasting impact that would honor the past while educating the future. Being a Girl Scout for 12 years, she felt ready to take on the responsibility of being the keeper of these local legends.

Compelling Truth

When it came time to decide on the format for her project, Erica initially felt that a physical book was the most powerful choice. She believed that a book would be more accessible than a simple website because it would allow readers to flip through history physically, seeing the progression of conflicts from World War II to the modern struggles in Afghanistan and Iraq. She wanted to include maps and high-quality photos so that the readers could visualize exactly where these service members had stood. However, Erica soon realized that her project could be even more immersive if she used technology, so she decided to create a website to accompany the book. This website allowed her to share something a book never could: the actual audio recordings of her interviews. She knew that hearing the emotion in a veteran's voice would provide a more in-depth research experience than a simple transcript.

Erica had always loved to write, but most of her experience before this project had been in fiction. This project forced her to grow into a different kind of author, one who worked with primary source material and meticulous details. She couldn't just use her imagination; she had to be accurate about dates, branches of service, and specific locations where these heroes were stationed. The writing process was long and required a deep level of focus to ensure she did justice to the stories she had been entrusted with.

Her first step in the writing process was transcribing the audio tapes she had recorded into a written format. As she listened to the hours of interviews, she found herself moved by the emotional weight of what the veterans shared. She decided she didn't want just to list facts like a dry report; she wanted to write compelling nonfiction that pulled readers in. She carefully analyzed each interview to find the most "crucial thing" a veteran said or an experience that could serve as an engaging opening for their chapter. This new approach to writing required more time and effort, but it produced a distinguished 84-page book that celebrated the unique spirit of everyone.

Memory Bridge

The project required Erica to build a strong team of professionals and volunteers who shared her dedication to the community. She reached out to her local historical society, which became an invaluable resource for finding contacts and setting high standards for her work. This partnership allowed her to move beyond her own circle of friends and connect with a broader network of veterans who were ready to share their truth.

To ensure her interviews were professional and legally sound, Erica followed a particular process guided by her team:

The Library of Congress Method: She used these official standards to conduct her interviews, ensuring she captured essential data like rank, branch, and title.

Official Release Forms: She learned the importance of legal documentation, having every veteran sign a form so their stories could be shared with the public.

Educational Outreach: She partnered with local elementary schools to bring history to life for the next generation.

Interactive Programming: She designed games and programs for seven and eight-year-olds to make the origins of Veterans Day and Memorial Day engaging.

Teaching the younger children was one of the most rewarding parts of her implementation plan. Initially, Erica struggled to find a way to make veteran issues feel relevant to kids who might not have service members in their own families. She decided to bring in games and books to make the lessons high-energy and fun. The moment of true success came when she held up a photo of one of the veterans she had interviewed, and a student shouted, "Oh, that's my neighbor! I didn't know he was a veteran!" This moment was a perfect example of her project's mission; it reminded the children—and even the adults—that veterans are everywhere, serving as our doctors, our teachers, and our neighbors. Erica had successfully turned "distant history" into a local connection that the kids could see every time they walked down their street.

Color And Costs

💰 💰 💰 💰 💰

As the project grew from a few interviews into a comprehensive 84-page book, Erica faced a logistical challenge: the cost of high-quality printing. She felt very strongly that she shouldn't "short-change" the photos and the colorful badges the veterans had shown her. She wanted the book to have glossy pages and bright, full-color images that these heroes deserved. However, printing a large, professional book was expensive, and she didn't have the funds to make it a reality at first. This roadblock forced her to step into the roles of fundraiser and business manager.

Erica didn't let the high price tag stop her mission; instead, she became incredibly resourceful. She organized multiple bake sales and reached out to her community to pre-sell copies of the book to raise the necessary money. This taught her that a successful leader is strategic and willing to work through the "negative feedback" or the silence that sometimes comes with asking for help. She learned that if one path is blocked, you find a different person to talk to or a new way around the problem. By the time she had enough money to send the book to the printer, she had gained a new level of confidence in her ability to manage a complex budget.

Another internal challenge Erica faced was learning the importance of documentation during the process. She realized that when she was in the middle of a veteran interview or a community event, it was easy to get "lost in the moment". While that was a wonderful feeling, she later wished she had been more vigilant about capturing more photos and videos of the journey itself. She learned that, for girls of her generation, these digital tools are among the most valuable tools for demonstrating a project's impact and sharing it with the world. She began to set aside specific time to sit down and figure out how to record the interactions she was having with people, from setting up poster boards around town to the final interviews. This growth in her organizational skills ensured that her final report to the council was as detailed and professional as the book itself.

Legacy Without Borders

The result of Erica's hard work was the creation of her town's very first Veterans Day celebration. She didn't just publish a book; she organized a panel where veterans could speak directly to the community, increasing awareness and honor for their service. Even when the pandemic hit, Erica remained dedicated, creating a socially distanced event that enabled her town to recognize its heroes safely. Her project had become more than just a requirement; it was a bridge into a passion she continued to pursue even after it was officially finished. She even used her interviews as the basis for a semester-long research paper at school, demonstrating how the project's skills could blend into her academic life.

Erica's growth as a leader was visible in her newfound confidence in public speaking. Years earlier, she had helped her troop create "National Thank You First Responders Day," where she had to stand before a "very serious panel" of the town board to propose the event. Those early experiences gave her the strength to speak to high-ranking West Point officials and the historical society board during her project. She learned that if you know your topic well and do your research, you can handle any interview or presentation with grace. Her advice to other girls is never to be afraid to expand their project beyond their original ideas, as there is always room to grow and find new ways to honor those who have given so much.

Looking to the future, Erica is determined to take her mission to the national stage. She dreams of creating a national organization that provides funding and resources for others—both within the organization and beyond—to interview veterans in their own communities. She realizes that as veterans from older conflicts become less accessible, the urgency to capture their stories only grows. Erica has proven that one girl with a recorder and a notebook can preserve a community's soul. She continues to write, knowing that her voice, and the voices she carries, have the power to make the world a more grateful and connected place.

Erica's journey reminds us that history is not just a collection of dates on a timeline, but a tapestry of individual lives that must be woven together with care. Just as a single thread might seem small, when it is combined with others, it creates a story strong enough to withstand the tests of time. By opening her heart and a book, Erica showed her community that the greatest way to honor the past is to listen to the present, ensuring that every hero has a seat at the table of our collective memory.

Chapter 5
Behind The Lens

Josie Banner (Ep 39)

The Creative Spark

Josie Banner was never one to shy away from a challenge, whether it was physical, academic, or creative. Long before she began her project, she had already established herself as a girl of discipline and determination. At the age of eleven, she earned her black belt in Taekwondo, an experience she described as intense but rewarding in every way. This early foundation of focus served her well as she entered the STEM Early College at NC&T. Following in her brother's footsteps, Josie chose this specialized high school because she found her middle school curriculum a bit too easy; she was a student who wanted to see if she could make it in a grueling environment where four years of high school are compressed into two, followed by two years of free college courses taught by actual professors.

This high-pressure academic background didn't stifle Josie's imagination; it fueled her desire to give back to her community in a way that celebrated the arts. When it came time to plan her Gold Award project, she knew she wanted to do something that promoted creativity. "I knew that I wanted to do something creative with my project," she reflected, noting that her first thought was to host an art camp. However, the path to leadership is rarely a straight line. Finding a venue for an art camp proved difficult, and the planning process started to feel "a little bit messy". Instead of letting the project crumble, Josie adapted her vision.

She realized that her interests in technology and storytelling could combine into something even more unique: a film camp. This pivot allowed her to utilize her skills from her 3D modeling and Python programming classes while addressing a need for creative outlets for younger children. Once she secured a partnership with the University of North Carolina at Greensboro (UNCG), her vision finally had a home. The university allowed her to use their Digital Media Commons, a high-tech space that offered all the digital resources her future campers would need to bring their stories to life. With the venue secured and her volunteers recruited, Josie was ready to transform from a student into a director, guiding a new generation through the magic of cinema.

Lights, Camera, Action

The culmination of Josie's hard work was a five-day summer camp she titled "Lights, Camera, Action." The camp's primary mission was to promote creativity among young adults and children while providing a deep dive into the fascinating world of film history. Josie didn't just want the kids to point a camera and press record; she wanted them to understand the "why" behind the images. She developed a massive curriculum

to ensure every day was packed with value, eventually creating a website to share her 127-slide PowerPoint and over 80 photos of the camp in action.
https://filmstudiescamp.wixsite.com/camphome

To make the project a success, Josie had to act as an educator, a technician, and a mentor all at once. She taught her students about the importance of creativity and explored film history at the local, general, and international levels. One of the most engaging stories she shared with her campers was about the very first film ever made. Created by Edward Muybridge in 1878, it was an animation of a horse running. This film was revolutionary because it was the first time humans realized that horses have two hooves off the ground at certain points while they run. This kind of trivia helped the campers see that film was not just entertainment, but a tool for discovery.

The project was carried out with a careful balance of history and hands-on technical training. Josie focused on providing campers with professional-grade tools to help them feel like real filmmakers. To keep the project organized and educational, she utilized several key elements:

Professional Hardware: She provided camcorders that the children used to film their own original segments.

Special Effects Technology: She set up green
screens so the students could experiment
with digital backgrounds.

Editing Software: She taught the campers how to
use Shotcut, a video editing program that
allowed them to cut and polish their final
projects.

Digital Sustainability: She launched a website to
host the curriculum, resources, and final
student films so the learning could continue
long after the camp ended.

The camcorders were an absolute hit. Josie
observed that "whenever they had the camcorders
in their hands, they never wanted to let them go".
Watching the children's faces light up as they
mastered the technology was a powerful moment
for her. She had successfully taken the complex
concepts she learned in her early college courses
and translated them into something accessible and
thrilling for elementary and middle school students.

The Race Against The Clock

Even with a perfect venue and a brilliant
curriculum, Josie hit a roadblock that almost stalled
her project entirely: she had no campers. Because
her project approval came through late in the
school year, she found herself trying to recruit
students just as summer break was beginning. As
a girl leading a major initiative for the first time, she

assumed that reaching out to her old middle school would be a simple and effective way to find participants. "I was kind of assuming that I would be able to send flyers for something as cool as a summer camp," she admitted. Unfortunately, her old school never responded to her requests.

The silence was discouraging. Josie realized she was up against strict rules governing how flyers could be distributed within the school system. With the clock ticking and the camp dates approaching, she had to think like a professional marketer. She learned quickly that in the world of community service, it isn't just about what you ask, but "know who to ask". She reached out to a trusted friend and asked for help getting the word out to a broader network. Through personal phone calls and direct networking, Josie eventually filled her camp roster. Still, the experience taught her a vital lesson: the importance of starting early and having a backup communication plan.

This challenge forced Josie to grow in her communication skills. She couldn't just be the "quiet and shy" girl her teachers had known in the past. She had to be persistent and vocal. This was a significant step for her, especially given that she had been working on her personal growth for years. For instance, while she had been writing a comic book for over a year and exploring hobbies like whitewater rafting and caving, those were often solitary or small-group activities. Running a camp required her to lead a large group of people and navigate the bureaucracy of a school district. By the time the first camper walked through the door at UNCG, Josie had already overcome the most challenging part of the project: the art of the "hustle."

Zooming In On Success

The impact of "Lights, Camera, Action" was immediate and visible in the smiles of every child who attended. Josie's favorite memories didn't come from a single event, but from "anytime that the campers were really excited about what they were doing". She found that providing them with a curriculum they cared about made her feel incredibly happy and validated as a leader. The camp was so successful that when it came time for the students to fill out their end-of-camp surveys, their only real complaint was that they wanted more. "They were saying, 'Make it a two or three week camp instead of just the five days,'" Josie recalled with pride.

The project's reach extended well beyond those five days in the digital media lab. A year after the project was completed, Josie's mother—who is also a teacher—informed her that one of her former students was still asking when the next camp would be held. Knowing that she had left such a lasting impression on a student's life was the proudest piece of the project for Josie. She not only taught them how to edit a video or use a green screen, but also "impacted their lives in a way that they're just so excited about learning more about creativity".

To ensure the project was sustainable and reached as many people as possible, Josie made sure her website was a comprehensive resource. It served as a digital archive of the camp's success, featuring:

- **Visual Documentation:** A gallery of 80 photos showing the kids working and playing.
- **Educational Access:** A link to the full 127-slide curriculum for other educators to use.
- **Future Resources:** Lists of software, like Shotcut, that students could download at home to keep practicing their skills. Josie felt this digital component was essential because it kept the "Lights, Camera, Action" mission alive. Even if she couldn't be there to host the camp every summer, the tools for creativity were now available to anyone with an internet connection.

The Final Cut

Reflecting on her journey, Josie realized that the project had fundamentally changed how she viewed herself as a leader. She had gone from a student who simply "got A's pretty easily" in middle school to a young woman who could navigate university partnerships, manage a team of volunteers, and inspire a room full of children. Her time at the STEM Early College provided the technical foundation, but the project provided the heart. She even found time to maintain her connection to her troop, occasionally visiting the trail bench she built for her community during her Silver Award project back in 2016.

As she prepared to graduate and head to UNCW in the fall, Josie had a clear vision for her future. She planned to double major in Film Studies and Computer Science, a perfect mirror of the two worlds she bridged during her camp. Her advice to other girls who are considering taking on a massive project of their own is simple: "Definitely know who to ask and also maybe start a little bit earlier on it". She emphasized that while the paperwork and planning can be a lot of work, the reward of seeing a project through to completion is "wonderful".

Josie Banner is a girl who respects tradition but isn't afraid to add her own creative flair, turning the ordinary into the spectacular. Whether she is double-majoring in college, publishing her first comic book, or eventually directing her first feature film, Josie has proven that she has the tools to succeed.

Josie's story reminds us that a project is like a film set—it requires a director who can handle the "messy" moments, a script that educates, and a lens that stays focused on the goal even when the lighting changes. By finding a way to share her passion for film, Josie didn't just earn an award; she developed a permanent reel of leadership skills that will play out across the rest of her life.

Chapter 6

The Voices of Silver Stories

Mikenna D. (Ep 147)

Living Libraries Of The Heart

Mikenna D. did not just happen upon her passion for helping seniors; she was practically raised in the warm, bustling hallways of a nursing home. Since the very day she was born, she had been a constant presence at a local care facility where her great-grandmother lived. Even after her great-grandmother passed away, Mikenna's family believed it was vital for her to keep returning every week to visit the residents. They wanted her to understand that older generations hold immense value and are essentially living libraries of human experience. To Mikenna, the people she met weren't just patients or residents; they became "her peeps" and her true friends.

As she grew into a teenager, she noticed a quiet but devastating problem in the world around her. Every time an older person passed away, their unique history, humor, and wisdom vanished along with them. She looked at her own generation, which was obsessed with capturing every second of life on social media. Yet, the most incredible stories in her community were being told to empty rooms or forgotten entirely. A specific memory of her own grandmother was the spark she needed for her mission. Her grandmother possessed a rare treasure: an old recording of her own mother telling a simple bedtime story. Mikenna realized that hearing a real, physical voice creates an emotional connection that a photograph or a written note simply cannot match.

This realization became the main driving force for her project, which she named "Silver Stories". She recognized that to really feel a connection to someone, hearing their voice is key. She wanted to bridge the gap between youth and older adults, ensuring that no story was left behind as time passed. Her goal was to record the authentic stories of seniors in her community and turn them into a professional podcast series. She envisioned a platform where these voices could live forever on the internet, inspiring anyone in the world. She was determined to give these seniors a voice that the world would finally listen to.

Mountain Of No

Starting the project was far more difficult than Mikenna ever imagined, feeling more like a climb up a mountain of red tape than a stroll. She quickly discovered that when you are working with a large organization or a vulnerable population, you cannot just walk in with a microphone and start recording. She had to navigate a complex maze of legalities, including complicated consent forms and "power of attorney" issues. Because she was still a high school student, these professional hurdles felt completely overwhelming. She admitted she wasn't naturally tech-savvy and didn't have a social media presence to help spread the word.

The biggest blow to her spirit came during the project approval process. Mikenna was one of those girls whose proposals were not accepted on the first try. In fact, her plan was rejected "several times" by the council because her vision wasn't clear or specific enough. The committee didn't just want a nice idea; they wanted to see the "big why" behind the work. They challenged her to find actual data to support her claims. When she told them that seniors were struggling with isolation, they responded with a tough question: "Where did you get that information?" They pushed her to find the statistics and logic to prove that senior isolation was a real community crisis that her project could help solve.

To get the proposal approved, Mikenna had to stop thinking in generalities and start focusing on the fine details of her mission.

- **Explaining the "How":** In her first draft, Mikenna simply wrote that she would "make a booklet." Her project advisor pushed back, asking exactly what that meant. Mikenna realized, "You can't just say that you're making a book. You have to explain how you're going to do that" in detail.
- **Problem-Solving the Budget:** Initially, she dreamed of using professional services for "the fancy booklets" so seniors could have a

high-quality copy of their story. However, the committee challenged her on how she would pay for it. She realized, "Wait, like that costs a lot of money. I can find a way to work around that".

- To keep the project affordable and repeatable, she decided to use her own computer and Google Slides to design the booklets herself.
- She then found a way to have them color printed at her school and stapled them together to create a professional-looking finished product.

- **Finding Real Evidence:** I went to a nursing home and found someone willing to help me find data to support my observations and make them reasonable.
- **Identifying the Project Plan:** Mikenna noted that "it really helped in the end to have everything planned out and get a better idea of what I was working on and why I was working on it".

Through this persistence, Mikenna transformed her project from a simple "nursing home visit" into a professional, data-backed mission that was ready to make a real impact.

This period was a test of Mikenna's resilience and persistence. She felt the sting of frustration every time she had to go back to the drawing board and rethink her strategy. Eventually, she realized the committee wasn't trying to be mean; they were trying to help her think through the logistics so the project would succeed. She learned how to balance her creative vision with the tedious reality of research and legal forms. She stayed insistent, refusing to let the word "rejected" stop her from helping her friends in the nursing home. Through this, she learned that a leader has the grit to keep going when the paperwork feels impossible.

Capturing Echoes

Once the proposal was finally approved, the real magic of the project began to unfold. Mikenna set out to record seven interviews, each offering a unique window into the history of the world. She met a World War II veteran, a Holocaust survivor, and people who simply had great jokes or a lifelong love for dancing. She discovered that the key to a great interview was making the environment feel informal and comfortable. Instead of a scary, high-pressure recording session, she would tell the seniors, "Hey, this is just to get to know you. Be authentic, be yourself, and just have fun with it". Soon, the seniors would forget there was even a microphone in the room and just start talking about their lives.

To make the project even more special, Mikenna wanted the participants to have a physical piece of their own legacy to keep. She decided to create personalized booklets for each senior, featuring their story and favorite photos. However, she hit another roadblock when she realized that high-quality, professionally printed photo books were far beyond her budget. Instead of giving up, she found a creative workaround using the resources she already had at school. She used her computer and Google Slides to design her own booklets from scratch, which she then printed and assembled herself.

Carrying out the project required a blend of technical skills and community partnerships that Mikenna had to manage all at once. She had to be a producer, a designer, and a historian to ensure the "Silver Stories" were preserved correctly. To keep the project organized and professional, she followed several key steps:

Partnered with two different local nursing homes to identify seniors who were eager to share their histories and life lessons.

Consulted with a legal mentor to ensure all consent forms and privacy protections were correctly handled for the vulnerable residents.

Utilized school resources to color-print the memorial booklets, ensuring each senior had a tangible copy of their legacy.

Established a dedicated YouTube channel to host the audio files, making the stories accessible to a global audience.

By the time she finished her seventh interview, Mikenna had logged over 80 hours of work. She realized that the tech side—the part she had been so afraid of initially—was fun once she got the hang of it. The trial-and-error of editing audio and building a website (https://sites.google.com/view/silver-stories-40202) taught her that she was capable of much more than she ever imagined. She was no longer just a girl visiting the nursing home; she was an entrepreneur and a community leader. She had successfully turned a small weekly visit into a professional digital archive.

A Bridge Across Time

The impact of "Silver Stories" extended far beyond the walls of local care centers. One of the most powerful moments of the project happened when Mikenna sat down with the family of a Holocaust survivor. The resident had memory problems and was very shy, so her son sat beside her to help tell her story. Mikenna listened in awe as he described how his mother had rescued a young boy while she was in a concentration camp. Even after all the terrible things that had happened to her during the war, she had remained brave, loving, and kind. Mikenna realized in that moment that people have stories far beyond the little homes and routines we are used to.

This specific story moved Mikenna so deeply that she decided to reach out to a teen author in Oregon named Claire. Claire had worked to change a law regarding Holocaust education and had met survivors herself. When the two connected, they realized that, even though they lived in different states, they were part of the same mission to remember these stories. This moment proved to Mikenna that her project was part of a much larger, global conversation about human rights and history. It was a beautiful moment when different generations and walks of life connected through the power of one story.

The project's success also opened doors to international recognition. After finishing her project, Mikenna entered a worldwide app-designing competition exclusively for girls. She decided to take her "Silver Stories" concept and design an app that would allow anyone to record and submit a senior's story to a digital collection. Out of thousands of entries from across the globe, Mikenna placed as a semi-finalist. This accomplishment showed her that her idea wasn't just a small local project; it was a solution that the whole world could use. She saw firsthand that her work could transform lives by ensuring no one feels alone in the world.

From Student To Leader

Completing the project was a transformational journey that changed Mikenna from the inside out. She learned that the mission was never about earning a pin or a certificate; it was about the people she met and the experiences she gained. Before starting, she thought her project was just a task to complete, but by the end, she realized it allowed her to become herself and discover what was truly important to her. She transitioned from being a girl who followed instructions to a leader who mentored others. She even began teaching younger girls about sportsmanship and entrepreneurship, serving as a role model just like her own leaders had been for her.

Mikenna's work with "Silver Stories" is far from over. She continues to interview seniors almost every week because she is dedicated to making the project bigger and better every year. Looking toward her future, she plans to attend Marquette University and is considering a nursing major. Her experience in the nursing home has given her a deep sense of compassion and a desire to continue serving the rest of her life. She hopes to one day become a leader for other girls, guiding them through their own journeys and helping them find their voices.

Mikenna's best advice for anyone starting their own project is to be yourself and be kind to others. She believes that even a simple smile can make a difference in someone's world. The project taught her that you might not always see the impact you are making in the moment, but if you keep persevering, you are sharing a light that cannot be extinguished. She realized that the "Silver Stories" were not just about the past; they were a roadmap for the future, showing her how to live with bravery and love. By giving a voice to those who felt forgotten, Mikenna found a powerful voice of her own.

Chapter 7

Uncovering Miss Kitty's Secret

Cee-Cee Deslaurier-Tate (Ep 154)

A Legend in the Dust

Cee-Cee Deslaurier-Tate grew up in Massachusetts, far away from the desert sun and the clicking spurs of the Old West, yet her heart always seemed to belong to a different century. Her journey into the past began when she was in the seventh grade, during a family trip to Tombstone, Arizona. To most people, it was just a vacation spot, but to Cee-Cee, stepping onto the main street of that authentic Old West town was a life-changing experience. She watched reenactors in heavy dresses and wide-brimmed hats, listened to the wood creak beneath their boots, and felt an immediate, magnetic pull toward the frontier's history.

When she returned home, the desert didn't leave her. She began reading every book she could find about that era and listening to the old *Gunsmoke* radio shows her uncle introduced her to. One night, while flipping through TV channels, she stumbled upon the television version of the show. An episode titled "Gold Mine" caught her eye, and there she saw her: Miss Kitty. Miss Kitty was unlike most female characters Cee-Cee had seen on old television shows; she was strong, independent, and held her own in a rugged, male-dominated world. Cee-Cee's parents had raised her on classic shows from the 1950s and '60s, but it was Cee-

Cee who became the true expert, eventually getting her whole family hooked on the series.

As her admiration for the character grew, Cee-Cee began to wonder about the woman behind the role—the actress Amanda Blake. She started digging into Blake's life, expecting to find the typical story of a Hollywood star. Instead, she uncovered a monumental secret: Amanda Blake had been a fierce, behind-the-scenes hero for animals. While celebrities like Betty White were famous for their animal advocacy, Amanda's work was mostly hidden from the public eye. Cee-Cee discovered that Amanda wasn't just an actress who liked pets; she was a world-class conservationist who had helped save entire species from extinction.

Cee-Cee had been in Girl Scouts for twelve years, and as she approached the time for her highest leadership project, she knew she had found her mission. She realized that Amanda Blake's story was a legacy that deserved to be shared with the world. Cee-Cee decided her project would be to honor this hidden hero, ensuring that the woman who played Miss Kitty was remembered for the lives she saved off-screen as much as the character she played on-screen.

Framing a Hidden Legacy

The scale of the project Cee-Cee envisioned was massive. She didn't want just to give a speech or make a poster; she decided to create a full-length documentary film. It was a commitment that would eventually demand over a thousand hours of her time. She knew the project had to be more than just a biography; it had to be a tool for conservation education.

At the core of Amanda Blake's secret life was a deep love for African wildlife. Cee-Cee's research led her to a book she won at an auction, *Serengeti Home*, which included a personal note from the author to Amanda. Through this and other documents, Cee-Cee learned that Amanda and her husband, Frank Gilbert, had established the very first captive breeding program for cheetahs at a time when the species was highly endangered. Their tireless research and hands-on work helped save the cheetah population in zoos worldwide. This incredible feat became the central pillar of Cee-Cee's documentary proposal.

However, Amanda's heart was as big as the Serengeti, and her work reached back to her home in Arizona as well. She co-founded the Arizona Animal Welfare League (AAWL) in 1971, the state's first and oldest no-kill shelter. She was a pioneer of the anti-euthanasia movement for dogs and cats, fighting for the lives of domestic animals decades before it was a popular cause. Cee-Cee realized she had to weave all these threads together—the Hollywood fame, the African plains, and the local shelters—to show the full span of Amanda's impact.

Planning such a project was an enormous undertaking for a high school student. Her final report alone would eventually reach 52 pages. She had to figure out how to condense a lifetime of heroism into a format that would keep an audience engaged. Her mentor warned her to stay on track and avoid trying to cover every detail of Amanda's life. Still, Cee-Cee found so much inspiration that the documentary eventually ran for 2.5 hours. She even included Amanda's personal battle with cancer, hoping that sharing the actress's bravery during her illness would inspire others facing their own health challenges. Cee-Cee was determined that every hour of her thousand-hour project would serve a purpose, turning a forgotten history into a living blueprint for future conservationists.

High-Stakes Balancing Act

Despite her passion, Cee-Cee faced a daunting reality: she was not a "tech person". Creating a documentary involves complex layers of technology that go far beyond just pointing a camera. She had to learn how to record professional voiceovers, edit photos into a sequence, and time music perfectly to evoke the right emotions. She spent nearly every day toward the end of her project at the local TV studio in her town, where the staff helped her master the equipment. Each time she walked into that studio, she faced a steep learning curve, teaching herself the technical skills needed to bring her vision to life.

The technical hurdles were only part of the struggle. During the final push to finish her project, Cee-Cee was navigating a high school schedule that was already bursting at the seams. She was taking several Advanced Placement classes through a virtual school, which meant she had to teach herself complex subjects without a teacher standing at the front of a classroom. At the same time, she was filling out college applications and writing pros and cons lists for different universities.

The pressure reached a boiling point when she landed a role in a theatrical production at the Stadium Theatre in Rhode Island. It was a radio show where Cee-Cee was the only woman in a small cast, requiring her to play 11 different parts with 11 distinct voices. She recalled being incredibly stressed, wondering, "How am I going to come up with these voices and do APs and college and the documentary?" It felt as though she was trying to juggle too many plates at once, and any one of them could come crashing down at any moment.

Cee-Cee had to become a master of time management. She wrote detailed schedules, carving out blocks of time for editing at the studio, practicing her 11-character voices, and studying for her exams. There were moments when the project felt impossible, like when work at the studio would accidentally be erased, or technical glitches would set her back. Yet, she refused to give up. She realized that when you choose a project you are passionate about, that attachment gives you the strength to push forward even when the path is difficult. She learned that she was more resilient than she ever imagined, discovering that her internal drive was stronger than any external obstacle.

Building a Bridge of Voices

A significant part of Cee-Cee's project involved reaching out to strangers to gather the stories that didn't appear in books or news articles. This was a massive communication challenge for a young woman, but she took it one step at a time. She began by contacting Beckey Burgoyne, the author of Amanda Blake's autobiography, *Perfectly Amanda*. Beckey had spent years traveling and interviewing people who knew the actress, and she was able to refer Cee-Cee to friends and colleagues who were still around to share their memories.

One connection led to another, and soon Cee-Cee was building a network of personal stories that showed the side of Amanda Blake the world didn't know. She was nervous before every interview, clutching her clipboard and checking her questions, but she was continually surprised by the people she met. She realized that even though these people had done amazing things in their careers and were friends with world-famous celebrities, they were "just like everybody else" when you sat down to talk with them. One of her favorite memories was a trip to Pennsylvania to interview one of Amanda's close friends; by the end of the day, they were all sitting on a patio together eating hamburgers, feeling like they had known each other for years.

To ensure the project made a lasting, measurable impact on the community, Cee-Cee didn't stop at the film. She wanted to create permanent markers of Amanda's legacy that people could see with their own eyes. To carry out this part of the project, she took several key actions:

Organized a fundraiser called "Amanda's Angels," where she made and sold corn husk dolls to raise money for a commemorative paving stone at the Phoenix Zoo.

Authored an article for the Phoenix Zoo's international newsletter, *Wild Times*, to share the story of Amanda's cheetah conservation work with experts around the globe.

Collaborated with the Arizona Animal Welfare League to install a memorial plaque featuring

Amanda's picture and a summary of her contributions as a co-founder.

Worked with the Phoenix Zoo auxiliary to ensure Amanda's name was added to the auxiliary's Armada plaque after years of being overlooked.

Cee-Cee also used modern tools to keep the community involved. She created a Facebook profile under the name "Kitty Russell" to track the documentary's progress and the memorials. https://www.facebook.com/KittyARussell# She committed to a "Weekly Post" every Monday to share updates with the thousands of fans worldwide who were waiting for the film's release. Through these various methods, Cee-Cee ensured that the "big why" of her project—honoring a forgotten hero—became a reality that touched people across the globe.

Walking in Her Boots

By the time Cee-Cee completed her project, she realized it had done more than just save a legacy; it had helped her discover who she truly was. She finished her documentary and earned recognition for her project right before leaving for her first year of college. Looking back on the thousand hours of work, she realized that the process had been life-changing. The confidence she gained from leading an extensive team of interviewees, studio staff, and organization leaders shaped her entire perspective on her future.

Today, Cee-Cee doesn't just talk about Miss Kitty; she has stepped into the role herself. Inspired by the strength she saw in Amanda Blake, Cee-Cee now works as a Kitty Russell tribute artist. On select weekends, she travels to places like Wild West City in New Jersey or Goldfield Ghost Town in Arizona, where she puts on her purple saloon dress and portrays the character for tourists and fans. She writes her own skits, introduces can-can dances, and shares the history of the Old West with the next generation. By portraying Miss Kitty, she keeps Amanda Blake's legacy alive in a vibrant, interactive way, combining her love for theater with her deep respect for the actress's values.

Cee-Cee's future is now firmly rooted in the path Amanda Blake paved for her. She continues polishing the documentary for its international release, knowing that fans from around the world are eager to see the results of her hard work. She credits the project with opening doors she never thought would open and helping her find her voice as an artist and an advocate. She remains grateful to her team, her parents, and the fans who supported her when the technical glitches made her want to give up.

The lesson Cee-Cee shares with others is simple: follow your heart and your passion. She learned that when you do something that really matters to you, you can achieve goals that seem impossible. Amanda Blake's secret life is no longer a secret, thanks to a girl from Massachusetts who was brave enough to dig into the past and bright enough to share it with the future. Cee-Cee didn't just tell a story; she became a part of it, ensuring that the kindness and bravery of a hidden hero will never be forgotten.

Chapter 8

Map the County's Local Harvest

Nicole Curristan (Ep 89)

Seeds Of A Vegan Visionary

Nicole Curristan's journey toward her highest project didn't start in a boardroom or a library; it began on her dinner plate. Growing up as a vegan in a semi-rural corner of East County, San Diego, Nicole was always more aware of her food than most of her peers. While other kids might just see a grocery store as a place where boxes of cereal magically appear, Nicole understood that every apple and every bunch of kale had a story. She had been part of her program since she was a five-year-old in kindergarten, learning about community service and the environment one step at a time. By the time she reached high school, her passion for the earth was no longer just a hobby—it was the core of who she was.

The real spark for her project ignited during a program journey called "Sow What?" when she was in the tenth grade. This wasn't just a regular school assignment; it was a deep dive into the world of local agriculture. Nicole learned about "food miles," the staggering distance a piece of fruit often travels before it reaches your kitchen. She discovered that when we buy food from thousands of miles away, it requires massive amounts of fuel and creates pollution that harms the planet. But the lesson that hit closest to home was the economic one. Nicole realized that when people buy food from local farmers, the money stays in their own community, helping small family businesses survive and thrive.

Inspired by this journey, Nicole and a friend decided to take action. They created a small guide that mapped out 5 to 10 farms in their local semi-rural community. They distributed the guide to their local chamber of commerce, and the response was terrific. But as Nicole looked at the map of her tiny neighborhood, a bigger idea began to take root. She looked at the sprawling map of San Diego County and thought, "What if I did this for the whole region?" She naively assumed that most of the farms were just in her backyard and there wouldn't be many more elsewhere. She had no idea that she was about to embark on a massive undertaking that would map an entire county and change the way her neighbors thought about their food.

County-Sized Challenge

When Nicole decided to expand her tiny neighborhood guide into a county-wide resource, she quickly realized she had vastly underestimated the scale of the job. San Diego County is enormous, and it turns out to be home to a massive number of small-scale farms. Nicole's goal for her project, titled "Eating Local San Diego," was to build a comprehensive website that would act as a one-stop shop for anyone looking to support local agriculture. She wanted to include addresses, maps, and even videos of the farms so that people could feel a personal connection to the people growing their food.

Just as she was getting started, the world changed. The COVID-19 pandemic hit, and the "old way" of doing things—like going out and interviewing farmers in person or handing out flyers at community events—was no longer safe. Nicole had to rethink everything. As a girl who preferred to be out in her community, being stuck behind a computer screen was a major hurdle. "I really wanted to kind of initially go out there and talk to people," she reflected, but the health of her community had to come first.

Since the project was so big, Nicole faced what she called "month-long lulls". There were times when the sheer amount of data she had to sort through felt overwhelming. She would look at her spreadsheet of hundreds of farm addresses and wonder if she would ever finish. She admitted that she sometimes put the work off for weeks just to catch her breath. However, her commitment to the farmers who were struggling kept her going. She knew these small businesses needed community support, and her website could be the tool that helped them stay afloat. She pushed through the lulls, drafting hundreds of emails and reaching out to local chambers of commerce to see who could help her spread the word digitally.

Building The Digital Barn

The project required Nicole to transform from a student into a researcher and a web designer. She had to learn technical skills she had never used before, such as purchasing a domain and organizing complex maps. Her primary tool was Google Sites, which she chose because it allowed her to "drag and drop" elements, but even then, the learning curve was steep. She spent hours watching YouTube tutorials and reading "how-to" articles to figure out how to make the site look professional and easy to navigate.

To ensure the information on the site was accurate and helpful for actual farmers, Nicole partnered with an expert advisor who was a local farmer herself. This advisor gave Nicole the "ins and outs" of the industry, teaching her how to describe various farming practices and what the public needed to know to support small farms.

Nicole managed the project by breaking it down into specific steps:

Data Categorization: She built a massive spreadsheet where she categorized hundreds of addresses and farm specialties by region.

Stakeholder Outreach: She drafted and sent hundreds of professional emails to chambers of commerce and farm alliances to verify information.

Web Design and Beta Testing: She used Google Sites to build the platform and had friends and family "beta test" the font sizes and navigation to ensure it was user-friendly.

Global Integration: She submitted her findings to the California Alliance for Family Farmers and added her data to a statewide database, where it still exists today. https://caff.org/directory/

Nicole's dedication to detail was exhausting but rewarding. She spent the winter and the spring meticulously entering data. One of her proudest moments was when she finished the maps that allowed users to find a farm near them with just a few clicks. She also included resources on the environmental impact of small farms, explaining how their sustainable practices are better for soil and water than those of giant industrial operations. Her project was no longer just a list of names; it was a digital ecosystem designed to sustain the community she loved.

The Advocacy Ripple Effect

As the website "Eating Local San Diego" went live, the impact began to ripple outward in ways Nicole never expected. Because she was serving as a national delegate for her council during this time, she was surrounded by other volunteers and leaders who were eager to share her work. One of her fellow delegates shared the website with her husband, who happened to be a science teacher in San Diego. He was so impressed that he showed the entire project to his whole class. Hearing that young people were engaging with her website and learning about the science of agriculture was one of Nicole's favorite memories. "That was so heartwarming to hear and like exactly what I wanted to hear," she said.

Nicole realized that education didn't have to stop with her website. She felt a need for more environmental connection, so she completed an online journey called "Girltopia". This experience led her and her mentor, Anne Fege, to create a brand-new advocacy group called Girls for Environmental Action, or GEA. They launched monthly Zoom meetings to teach other girls about food waste, water use, and plastic pollution.

This new group grew rapidly, eventually reaching a leadership team of nine people. They even started a summer internship program where older girls could design workshops for younger participants. Nicole had successfully turned her individual project into a movement. By making environmental education accessible via Zoom, she ensured that girls from across San Diego and Imperial counties could participate, regardless of where they lived.

Her work proved that even when we are physically separated, a shared passion for the planet can build a powerful, virtual sisterhood. She wasn't just helping people find local tomatoes anymore; she was training the next generation of environmental leaders.

Cultivated In Leadership

Reflecting on the two years she spent on her project, Nicole realized that she had grown just as much as the crops on the farms she mapped. She learned that being a leader doesn't mean having a perfect plan from day one; it means being flexible enough to change when things aren't working. She recalled that early on, she was self-conscious about her work and didn't like people reading what she had written. However, the process taught her to shed that fear and embrace constructive criticism. "I kind of learned to shed that and really just tried to realize that when I get kind of criticism... that's how I create the best product," she explained.

Her time as a national delegate further sharpened her leadership. She spent months nitpicking the language of proposals and understanding the "sheer enormousness" of the organization she belonged to. This high-level experience gave her the confidence to talk to anyone, from local farmers to state-wide alliances. She advises other girls to "just keep going and just try it," even when they hit those long lulls. She learned that adults in the community truly want to see young people succeed and are more than willing to help if you just reach out.

As she heads off to the University of California, Los Angeles (UCLA), Nicole has a clear path forward. She plans to major in environmental science and minor in environmental engineering and conservation biology. She's even looking forward to joining the Daily Bruin, the student newspaper, to continue her love of writing and advocacy. Although she is leaving her local council for a new one in Los Angeles, she can't imagine leaving the program behind. Nicole knows that the skills she cultivated—the persistence, the digital savvy, and the ability to listen—are the tools she will use for the rest of her life.

Nicole's story shows us that a project is much like a garden. It requires a girl who is willing to clear the weeds of doubt, plant the seeds of a big idea, and patiently water them through the long lulls of a pandemic. While the website she built is a permanent digital harvest for San Diego, the real fruit of her labor is the confidence she now carries—a confidence that will bloom in every classroom and every community she enters for years to come.

Chapter 9
Reporting For Change

Grace Gromley (Ep 128)

Newsroom Diversity Gap

Grace Gromley was a student who understood the immense power of the written word. She had been a dedicated member of the journalism community in her high school for years and was entering her third year of reporting when she began her mission. Her public high school was a vibrant, diverse place she loved dearly, yet she noticed a troubling trend in the media center's hallways. Even though her journalism program was massive, with more than 100 students participating, the staff did not reflect the beautiful diversity of the greater school population. This lack of representation bothered Grace because she knew that journalism is the lens through which we all view our world. She believed that if there were ever a strike in the industry, no one would have any idea what was happening in their own neighborhoods. This imbalance was a problem she was determined to fix with her highest leadership project.

Grace realized that for many underserved students, journalism felt distant or intimidating. She theorized that if she could introduce these kids to the craft at a younger age, they could build the skills and confidence needed to join the high school program later. She wanted to give them the tools to speak up for their communities through a project she titled "Speak Up: Standout Journalism for Young Activists". Her background in the journalism program had taught her that telling stories is a way to represent a community in fun and powerful ways. By focusing on activism, she hoped to show younger students that their opinions mattered.

Grace's motivation came from her own passion for storytelling and screenwriting, which had always been a way for her to express herself. She knew from her own family's experiences that being part of a newsroom could provide a sense of joy and power. However, she didn't want that power limited to just one group of people. She was ready to take on the challenge of building a bridge between middle schoolers and the high school newsroom. Her ultimate goal was to ensure that high-quality, balanced, and responsible reporting remained a cornerstone of her community's future. She began planning a free summer camp to turn middle schoolers into mini-journalists, ready to take on the world.

Building The Summer Newsroom

Grace started her project with a modest goal: she wanted to host a summer camp for about 25 children. She spent hours developing a custom curriculum based on the "Beginning Journalism" class she had taken herself. She reached out to her peers, successfully recruiting a dozen high school students to volunteer their summer days as

counselors. To find her students, she partnered
with a local organization called Dreamcatchers,
which provides one-to-one tutoring for underserved
kids in her district. She met with the executive
director and explained her vision for the camp.
They were immediately impressed and asked if the
camp could become a permanent part of their
official summer program.

While Grace was thrilled by the support, she was
also hit with a sudden, massive challenge. Instead
of the 25 students she had planned for,
Dreamcatchers had 70 students who needed
instruction. Suddenly, Grace had triple the number
of students but only 12 counselors, and absolutely
no money for supplies. She admitted that the first
day was terrifying, and she walked into the building
with her stomach in knots. She looked at the
dozens of sixth through eighth graders running
around and wondered if she could ever get them to
focus on the lessons. She knew she had to get her
game together quickly to avoid being overwhelmed.

To handle the surge in students, Grace had to
become a master of delegation. She worked with
the tutors she had already trained and "deputized"
them to teach the other Dreamcatchers volunteers.
She applied for community grants and sought local
sponsorships to fund the printing of the magazines
the students would create. This was a growth step
for her, as she had to learn to feel comfortable
letting other people take ownership of the project.
She realized that by the end, the project wasn't just

hers anymore; it belonged to everyone involved. Through this process, she learned that leadership is about trusting your team to help carry the load.

Interviews To Inky Pages

The camp ran for four weeks and was a whirlwind of creativity and hard work. Grace divided the 70 students into five different classrooms based on their grades. She drew on her own high school experiences to ensure the lessons were fun and accessible for middle schoolers. Her journalism teacher, Mr. Wilson, served as her project advisor and helped her adapt complex high school concepts into shorter, more engaging versions for a younger audience. She created Google Slides for every lesson, complete with notes so that any of her tutors could stand up and lead the class with confidence.

The kids didn't just sit and listen to lectures; they were active reporters from day one. They learned the technical side of the job, including how to compose professional photos and conduct effective research for their stories. They even practiced the art of the interview by questioning each other in class. Grace was amazed by the topics the students chose to cover, which ranged from serious global issues like climate change, teen homelessness, and deforestation to lighthearted features about Hot Cheetos and famous soccer players.

To ensure the project was carried out successfully, Grace followed a strict set of operational steps:

Recruited and trained a dozen high school peers to act as lead counselors and teaching assistants.

Developed a website to host her journalism curriculum, schedules, and tips so other teachers across the nation could recreate the camp. https://susocamp.weebly.com/

Managed a mad dash to the local printers to ensure that every student received a physical copy of their published magazine by the end of the term.

The program culminated in a student showcase where the young reporters read their articles aloud to their peers and families. It was incredibly meaningful for Grace to see the joy on the kids' faces when they finally held their printed magazines. One of the best parts was when students asked her if they were "really" allowed to write about things they cared about. Grace was able to look them in the eye and say "yes," because that is the beauty of journalism. These kids, many of whom had spent their entire morning in summer school before coming to her camp, were excited to see their high school teachers every single day.

The Fourth Of July Clock

Even the best-laid plans encounter speed bumps, and Grace's project was no exception. Because the camp lasted four weeks, she had only 10 days of actual instruction to guide all 70 students through brainstorming, researching, writing, and designing. The biggest hurdle appeared near the end of the project during the Fourth of July weekend. Grace had a strict deadline to get the articles to the printers, but because of the holiday, the shop informed her that she had to submit everything a day earlier than she had anticipated.

This news triggered a "mad dash" for Grace and her team. She had to immediately look at her curriculum and figure out what could be cut to make room for the new deadline. She decided to remove a photography lesson and moved up the period where the students finished their outlines. She spent hours designing layouts for every student article, ensuring the magazines would look professional and beautiful. This experience was a lesson in flexibility for someone who considered herself a "schedule person," living by her lists and calendar.

Grace learned that even if her plans were a little messed up, she could still succeed by adapting on the fly. She realized that persistence and resilience were required for any major leadership project.

Instead of viewing the printer deadline as a roadblock, she treated it as a simple speed bump. This shift in mindset made her school life much less stressful, as she now knew she could handle problems that weren't insurmountable. The ability to stay calm and adjust her plans became one of the most important skills she gained during the entire process. She proved that she could produce a high-quality product even when the timeline was working against her.

Editor-In-Chief's Legacy

By the time the final magazines were handed out, the impact of Grace's project was undeniable. She had successfully introduced dozens of underserved students to a world they might never have explored otherwise. To ensure the camp didn't end when she left for college, Grace created a permanent digital resource. She worked with Dreamcatchers to build a website that contains her entire curriculum, schedules, and various tips and tricks she gathered while running the camp. She shared this link with journalism teachers across the country, providing them with a blueprint to grow their own programs.

Grace's growth as a leader continued long after the summer sun set on her camp. She eventually rose to become the Editor-in-Chief of *Viking* magazine, which she describes as the best high school sports magazine in the country. In this role, she uses the confidence and leadership skills she honed during her summer project to lead a classroom of her peers. She helps her staff members find their own voices and encourages them to go deeper into their reporting. Grace has personally written powerful articles about athletes with disabilities and how menstruation affects female athletes, proving her commitment to inclusion.

Today, as she prepares for college, Grace remains a staunch advocate for responsible, balanced journalism. She still uses the persistence and flexibility she learned during those hectic summer weeks to manage her schoolwork, her swim team schedule, and her duties as an editor. She credits her project with helping her find a sense of control and joy in her busy life. Grace believes that anyone who wants to earn a Girl Scout Highest Award should stay persistent and always keep an eye on what motivates them. She is proud to have left her community better than she found it, one reporter at a time.

Chapter 10
Hidden History

Nell Murphy (Ep 97)

The Story Textbooks Forgot

Nell Yukiye Murphy sat in her high school history class, her eyes scanning the pages of her Advanced Placement U.S. History textbook. She was looking for a specific name, a specific place, or even a specific paragraph that reflected her own family's journey through the 1940s. What she found, however, was a deafening silence. In a book that was supposed to cover the entirety of American history, there was less than a single paragraph dedicated to the incarceration of Japanese Americans during World War II. There was absolutely no mention of Manzanar, the place where her grandfather had been forced to live behind barbed wire.

To Nell, this wasn't just an oversight in a curriculum; it was a missing piece of her own identity. She knew that her grandfather hadn't been a criminal or a threat to national security. He was put in block 13 of the Manzanar camp simply because of his heritage. There were no suspicions around him; he was an American citizen whose only "crime" was being of Japanese descent during a time of fear and war. Nell realized that if her high-level history book—the one being read by thousands of students—couldn't find the space to tell this story, then a whole generation was growing up without knowing the truth about this dark time in American history.

The motivation for her project hit her with the force of a landslide. She knew she had a deep, personal connection to this history that most of her peers lacked. If the textbooks weren't going to teach students about the barracks, the mess halls, and the daily lives of those held at Manzanar, then she would have to build the classroom herself. She didn't want to create something dry and intimidating; she wanted an easy, engaging way for people to learn. This spark led to the birth of "Journey to Manzanar," a project designed to take the world on a virtual tour of the very ground her grandfather once walked as a prisoner. She was determined to ensure that the stories of Block 13 would never be erased again.

Mapping The Memory

Once Nell knew her "why," she had to figure out the "how." She envisioned a virtual education platform where someone could sit at a computer and navigate through the historic site of Manzanar as if they were standing there in person. She knew that visual elements were the key to making history feel real, especially for younger people. She didn't want just old, grainy black-and-white photos that looked like they belonged in a dusty archive; she wanted something vibrant and immersive.

Building a virtual tour of a national historic site is a massive job for anyone, let alone a high school junior. Nell knew she needed to reach big and partner with organizations that had the power to make her vision a reality. She decided to "shoot for the stars" and approached the Eastern Sierra Interpretive Association (ESIA), a large organization that works closely with national parks. She also connected with the park rangers at the Manzanar National Historic Site. These were people she had known since she was a baby because her family was so involved in the community, but pitching them a professional project was still a nerve-wracking step into a leadership role.

She began having monthly Zoom meetings with Jeff, the head of the ESIA, to coordinate the technical side of the platform. The partnership was a dream come true: Nell would provide the research, activities, and content, while the ESIA would serve as the "home" for her project on its website. She also relied heavily on Ranger Alisa Lynch, who knew Nell's grandfather's history. Alisa helped Nell sift through old family documents, like the family number her grandfather had been forced to use. She ensured that Nell's vocabulary in the project was both accurate and respectful. With her team in place, Nell was no longer just a student with a grievance; she was a girl with a professional roadmap to change how history was taught.

Documenting History

Carrying out the project required Nell to become a fundraiser, a producer, and a researcher all at once. She realized that to get the high-quality video and photos she needed, she couldn't just use her phone. She recruited Juan, a family friend and professional cinematographer, to join her team. However, professional talent requires professional funding. Nell launched a letter-writing campaign, reaching out to friends, family, and members of the Japanese American community who shared her passion for preserving this history. Even though not everyone replied, she ended up raising far more than her original budget, proving that when you care about a cause, you can make others care, too.

With the funds secured, Nell and Juan traveled to the high desert of California for a two-day film shoot at the Manzanar site. They walked through the reconstructed barracks, the desolate bathrooms, and the vast mess halls, capturing the place's emptiness and weight. Nell acted as the guide, taking photos of everything that stood out to her as if she were seeing it for the first time. To ensure the project was executed perfectly, Nell followed several key operational steps:

Conducted deep-dive research into the archives at Manzanar with Ranger Alisa Lynch to find her grandfather's specific family records.

Filmed and edited dozens of short video sequences of less than a minute each to make the virtual tour fast-paced and engaging.

Designed corresponding educational activities for each exhibit to make sure visitors were absorbing the information they saw.

Every photo and paragraph was carefully chosen to "honor the people that went to these camps as opposed to exploiting them," a balance the rangers helped her maintain. She spent hours organizing the massive footage files, sifting through what worked and what didn't. The final result was a "preserved time box" of the camp, turned into an interactive game and tour that could reach people thousands of miles away. Nell wasn't just recounting the past anymore; she was using modern tools to give the ghosts of Manzanar a digital voice that would never be silenced. https://sierraforever.org/journey-to-manzanar/

Fighting The Skeptics

Even with a professional film crew and a national partnership, the path to finishing her project was blocked by unexpected hurdles. One of the strangest challenges Nell faced was convincing the project review committee that her idea was valuable. Because her project was virtual, some of the organization's adult volunteers didn't quite understand what a "virtual tour" would look like or why it was better than a traditional community service event. During her initial interview, the support was low, and she felt she had "a lot to prove".

Nell also felt the heavy weight of being a representative for an entire community. While she is Japanese American, she is also three-quarters white, and she struggled with the pressure of being the "sole representative" for a group of people who had suffered so much. She didn't want to speak *for* everyone who had been in the camps, but she knew she had to speak *up* because no one else was. This internal struggle, combined with a demanding high school schedule, meant that Nell eventually missed her intended project deadline by two months. She had to wait another six months just to have her final ceremony.

Nell refused to rush the work just to meet a date on a calendar. She chose to wait so she could produce "really good work," and that persistence paid off. When she finally walked into her closing interview, the atmosphere had changed entirely. The same people who had been skeptical at the beginning were now blown away by the "gorgeous project" she had built. One volunteer even told her she should contact local news outlets because the work was so incredible. By sticking to her vision and refusing to settle for a "not as decent project," Nell proved that a girl's passion can turn doubt into a standing ovation.

Standing In The Spotlight

The impact of "Journey to Manzanar" didn't end when the website went live. The platform became a sustainable educational resource hosted by the ESIA, ensuring that any student in any state could learn the history that Nell's textbook had skipped. For Nell, the project was a bridge between her family's past and her own future. She discovered that when you tackle a problem you genuinely care about, the logistics and hard work feel less like chores and more like a mission. She realized she had the power to make everyone else care about what mattered to her.

Nell is taking that same drive and "grit" to Carnegie Mellon University, where she is studying in their prestigious acting program. Her life has shifted from the high desert to the stage, where she spends her days in a conservatory environment, taking eight classes and earning 45 credits. She admits that the change is drastic, but she has found a new "built-in best friends" community among her fellow actors. She hopes to one day act professionally on screen, but her connection to her heritage remains a top priority. She still dreams of working at the Japanese American National Museum in Los Angeles during her summers.

Nell encourages other girls to take action in their communities, even if they aren't working toward a specific award. She believes that even small changes can bring about shifts in the world when driven by truth and passion. Nell's journey taught her that she was "braver than you believe, stronger than you seem, and smarter than you think". She didn't just build a website; she built a legacy for her grandfather and for every American who deserves to know the whole story. She proved that while a textbook might only give a topic a single paragraph, a girl with a camera and a purpose can give it the entire world.

Chapter 11

The Power of the Silent Word

A Heart Settled on Change

📚📚📚📚📚

Amani Ward was just a high school freshman when a single book shifted the entire trajectory of her life. Sitting in her World Literature class, she began to read *Speak* by Laurie Halse Anderson. The story follows a girl who is raped at a high school party and becomes an outcast, losing her voice to the trauma and the silence of those around her. As Amani turned the pages, she didn't just see a character; she saw a reflection of a silent epidemic that was haunting the hallways of high schools, middle schools, and college campuses everywhere.

What truly "settled in her heart" was not just the story itself, but the letters the author received afterward, which were included in the back of the book. Many of these letters came from males who were confused, asking why the character was so distraught after the incident. This lack of understanding—this fundamental gap in empathy and knowledge—horrified Amani. She realized that people were going through these traumatic experiences in total isolation, and their peers didn't even understand the basic effects of the trauma.

Right then, she decided she would not be another bystander. She knew she wanted to dedicate her project to bringing awareness to sexual assault, sexual harassment, and sexual peer pressure. She felt a profound responsibility to educate her peers, hoping to give them the tools to recognize signs of danger and the courage to speak up if the unthinkable happened. It was no longer just a school assignment or a requirement for her youth organization; it was a mission to ensure that no one else had to hide their story in the shadows.

Her personal motivation was rooted in the belief that "starting the conversation" was the only way to break the cycle. She wanted to reach out to high schoolers, middle schoolers, and even college students who were navigating a world filled with new social pressures. By combining her passion for film with her desire for advocacy, she began to outline a plan that would eventually reach far beyond the walls of her high school.

Advocacy Film Production

Amani was already enrolled in a film course at her school and decided to use her technical skills to create a professional documentary-style video. She wanted a resource that could show the signs of how to know if someone has gone through an assault or the red flags that it might happen in the future. However, Amani knew that a project this serious required a strong team behind her. She didn't just want to be a student behind a camera; she wanted to be a leader who brought the community together.

Her team was an impressive assembly of local figures and mentors. Her mother was her primary support, helping her with every project she had ever tackled. Her high school principal, Cooksey Misty, didn't just permit the project; she appeared in the video as an interview subject. Principal Misty even committed to using the video as a permanent resource at the school so that if a student ever came forward, they would have a clear place to turn. Amani also relied heavily on her troop leader, Paula, who was not only familiar with Amani's journey but also worked with the regional committee.

To bring the documentary to life, Amani had to manage several complex technical and logistical steps:

Equipment Management: She borrowed high-end filming equipment from her school's film department to ensure each interview's production value was top-tier.

The Learning Curve of Editing: While she was comfortable behind the lens, she had to undergo an intensive learning process to master post-production editing, working alongside an expert to piece the final story together.

Cross-Sector Networking: She coordinated with various organizations, including "Diamond in the Rough," to gather expert perspectives and group interviews.

Digital Resource Building: She developed a dedicated website, startingtheconversation.world, to host her video and provide accessible resources to anyone with an internet connection.

The filming process was a "breeze" for Amani because of her love for television and film production, but the editing was where the real work happened. She spent hours meticulously cutting footage and ensuring the message was both clear and sensitive. When the video was finally finished, it wasn't just a classroom project; it was a polished, powerful documentary that was ready to be shared with the world via YouTube and her own website.

Price of a Promise

⏳ ⏳ ⏳ ⏳ ⏳

Even with a strong team and a clear vision, the road to completing her project was paved with personal sacrifices. Amani was a junior in high school, a year that many students consider the most difficult. She wasn't just working on her advocacy project; she was buried under a "swamp" of work from difficult classes like Honors Physics and Honors British Literature. The first semester had gone smoothly, and she managed to get all her filming done, but when the second semester hit, the pressure became nearly unbearable.

Amani reached a turning point where she had to decide what truly mattered. Most juniors look forward to their prom as a highlight of their high school experience, but Amani saw her project deadline approaching and knew she couldn't do both. With a maturity that few of her peers possessed, she made the difficult decision to "forfeit going to my junior prom". She chose to stay focused on her grades and her mission to help victims of assault, proving that her commitment to the community was stronger than her desire for a dance.

Beyond the academic pressure, there were logistical hurdles that tested her patience. Scheduling interviews with busy professionals like her principal was a constant game of "phone tag" or last-minute changes. On the original date set for the principal's interview, an emergency involving a student required immediate attention, forcing Amani to reschedule and adapt. She learned quickly that being a leader meant rolling with the punches and remaining flexible when things didn't go according to plan.

Distance was another challenge. One of the organizations she wanted to work with, "Diamond in the Rough," was located a very long distance away from her home. To get the group interview she needed, she had to manage the travel and time logistics, further adding to her already packed schedule. Despite being swamped and tired, her troop leader, Paula, was "always on her back," checking in every two weeks to ask about her progress. This constant push from her mentor helped Amani keep her "ducks in a row" and ensured she reached the finish line despite the honors-level workload.

Voice on the Panel
🎤🎤🎤🎤🎤

As the project grew, Amani found herself stepping into a new role: that of a public representative for her generation. She was invited to sit on a panel alongside adults to discuss the realities of sexual assault from every possible angle. Her role was to represent the younger age group and explain why it was so difficult for teenagers to talk to the adults in their lives. Amani spoke eloquently about the "big age gap" between the current generation of students and their parents or teachers.

She pointed out that teenagers today live in a completely different world because of technology. "Back then," she explained to the panel, "you just had a phone to call somebody and just gossip, and that was it". Today, however, students carry their entire social lives in their pockets through laptops and social media. This creates a much "bigger threat" for victims to be exposed or shamed online, which keeps many of them silent. By bridging this gap, Amani helped the panel's adults understand the unique fears that keep her peers from seeking help.

The panel didn't just focus on the problems; it focused on the process of healing. They discussed what happens when a victim does choose to tell someone, covering everything from going to a hospital for a rape kit to filing a lawsuit against a perpetrator. Amani emphasized the importance of therapy, telling her audience that talking to a professional is the only way to "become somewhat yourself again" after a trauma. She was no longer just a girl with a camera; she was a vital, life-saving source of information.

This experience on the panel, combined with various events she held at colleges, allowed Amani to see "every aspect" of the issue. She learned that sexual assault "could happen to anyone". This deep dive into the research made her more aware of her own surroundings and the dangers of things like sex trafficking, which were becoming more prominent in the news. Her project had evolved from a response to a book into a comprehensive education for herself and her entire community.

Legacy of Healed Voices

The impact of Amani's project hit home during an event she held at a local college. After screening her video and discussing it with psychology and forensics teachers, a student came to Amani with a heavy secret. The student revealed that she had been a victim of sexual assault not just once, but twice. She told Amani that the video had given her the strength she needed, and for the first time in her life, she felt she could finally "talk to somebody about it".

For Amani, that testimony proved that her sacrifice of prom and her countless hours of editing were worth it. She had successfully "started the conversation". As she reached the end of her high school career, having been involved in Girl Scouts since she was a six-year-old Daisy, she felt that a chapter was closing. She had moved from raising money for pet beds as a child to saving lives through documentary filmmaking.

Looking toward the future, Amani has already been accepted into Clayton State University, where she plans to major in film and television. Her dream is to become a film director or a film editor, using her creative talents to continue telling stories that matter. She has learned that she is "capable of doing amazing things," a realization that has given her the confidence to pursue a high-stakes career in the media industry.

Amani's journey is a reminder that silence is a wall that can only be broken by the courage to speak. Her project was like a stone thrown into a quiet pond; the initial "conversation" was the splash, but the impact—the healing of victims and the education of peers—continues to ripple outward, touching lives she may never even meet. Through the lens of her camera, Amani turned a "foreign" and scary topic into a bridge of hope, proving that one girl's heart for change can lead an entire community toward the light.

Chapter 12
Life-Saving Choices

Srishti Gowda (Ep 40)

Waiting For Life

Srishti Gowda was always an observant and active student, but her perspective on the world changed forever when she was in the eighth grade. She watched her favorite English teacher go through a grueling journey that most people never see. Her teacher was waiting for a kidney transplant, a process that required her to change her entire life and schedule around a single, life-saving need. Srishti learned that her teacher had been waiting for three or four years, which is an incredibly long time to live in uncertainty, wondering if a donor would ever be found. This experience opened Srishti's eyes to a topic that many people in her community simply weren't talking about. She realized that while organ donation could save lives, it was often treated as a "taboo" subject that people preferred to ignore.

Determined to understand more, Srishti dove into research and was stunned by the statistics she uncovered. She found that in the United States alone, over 120,000 people were currently waiting for a life-saving transplant. Even more heartbreaking was the discovery that 22 people pass away every single day because an organ does not become available in time. Srishti felt a deep, personal motivation to take action. She realized that while the problem was massive, the solution was surprisingly simple: literally every single person has the power to change those numbers. It was a beautiful realization that something that took only "two minutes at most" could save a life.

As she moved into high school and began thinking about her project, Srishti knew she had to build upon this passion. She had already been a dedicated Girl Scout for years, earning her Bronze Award and Silver Award by helping her community and school. For her Bronze Award, she helped install a dog waste sanitation station to keep her school playground clean. For her Silver Award, she created a welcome packet for incoming sixth graders to help them navigate the scary transition to middle school, covering everything from lunch schedules to locker-opening tips. These experiences gave her the skills to manage a team and execute a plan, but her Gold Award would be her most ambitious mission yet. She didn't want to just "get it over with"; she wanted her project to have an "everlasting impact" on how people viewed the gift of life.

Driver's Seat

When Srishti started her own driver's education classes to get her license, she noticed a missed opportunity. When people go to the Secretary of State or DMV to get their license, they are asked if they would like to be added to the organ donor registry. However, Srishti realized that organ donation was barely mentioned in the actual driver's ed classes. Many teens simply checked "no" on the form because they didn't understand what it meant or because they believed common myths about the process. She knew that if she could target the teen demographic, she could reach the people who had the power to change everything. "Chances are if a teenager or a child finds out about organ donation and knows the truths... they're more likely to talk to their parents and their grandparents," she explained.

Srishti envisioned an improved education toolkit that would give young people the truths they needed to become heroes. To make this vision a reality, Srishti partnered with Gift of Life Michigan, the official organ procurement organization for her state. This partnership was crucial because it enabled her to update a toolkit that hadn't been updated in 8 to 10 years. She wanted to ensure the information was up to date and specifically targeted to students. Srishti spent long hours at her computer, creating documents that would speak directly to her peers. She put her "blood, sweat, and tears" into making the toolkit look professional and engaging.

The project was carried out with a sophisticated blend of digital and physical resources, designed to reach 84,000 students each year in her state. Srishti focused on making the material interactive so that it wasn't just another boring school presentation. To keep the project organized and educational, she utilized several key elements in her toolkit:

Direct Communication: She wrote specific letters for students and parents to help start the conversation about donation at home.

Teacher Support: She designed an informative flyer specifically for driver's ed instructors to help them guide the lesson easily.

Interactive Technology: She created an online Kahoot quiz that allowed students to test their knowledge in a fun, competitive way.

Educational Fact Sheets: She included informative flyers that summarized key facts and dispelled common myths.

Through this methodical approach, Srishti fostered effective education within her local Troy High community and beyond. She wasn't just handing out papers; she was creating a system of knowledge. She realized that by providing a starting point for these conversations, she was helping families prepare for difficult situations before they happened.

Power Of Personal Connection

Even with a perfect partnership and a brilliant toolkit, Srishti hit a roadblock that almost stalled her project: she couldn't get the schools to respond. Initially, she naively assumed that sending professional emails would be enough. She wrote up these emails saying, "Please fill out the survey. It will be a big help for me". To her disappointment, the response rate was incredibly low. As a girl leading an initiative for the first time, the silence from the driver's ed schools was discouraging. She realized that she was just another name in an overflowing inbox.

This challenge forced Srishti to grow in her communication skills. She learned that in the world of community service, people want to see a "personal connection with your project". She decided to pivot her strategy and start calling the schools personally. "I decided to start calling the drivers at schools personally and saying, 'Hey, I'm really passionate about this,'" she recalled. She explained why the topic was worth talking about and how it could save lives. This personal touch made all the difference. Once she showed her heart, she received a flood of responses from schools eager to use her materials.

This experience changed Srishti from a student following a plan into a persistent leader who knew how to "hustle" to make her vision a reality. She had to learn the "patience to sit down and say, 'What can I do differently?'" This flexibility helped her overcome the barrier posed by busy administrators. By the time her toolkit was being distributed across Michigan, Srishti had already overcome the most challenging part of the project—the art of finding her voice and using it to bring people together. She realized that most people actually "want to see you succeed" if you are willing to reach out and show your passion.

High-Stakes Challenge
🍕🍕🍕🍕🍕

One of the most exciting parts of Srishti's project was the high school challenge she organized in collaboration with Gift of Life Michigan. To get more young people involved, they created a competitive environment in which different high schools vied to sign up the most organ donors. The incentive was a pizza party for the winning school, which helped generate a lot of energy and passion among the students. Srishti spent her time at tables in the school media center, having one-on-one conversations with her peers and dispelling myths about donation. She found these personal interactions to be the most rewarding part of the entire project.

She loved watching "people's thoughts kind of turn" when she explained that you didn't have to be an adult to decide to save a life. Out of 26 schools participating in the challenge, Srishti's school, Troy High, placed fourth. Even though they didn't win the official pizza prize, Srishti was overjoyed to see

how many of her classmates became just as
passionate about the cause as she was. She
managed to sign up more than 150 people on the
registry at her school and in the surrounding
community.

Knowing that one organ donor can save up to eight
lives, Srishti realized her project could benefit
1,200 lives. This "full circle" moment helped her
see that the individual stories she heard from her
peers were part of a much larger, global impact.
She emphasized that the goal wasn't just about the
number of sign-ups, but about equipping the public
with information. "The goal is for people to take the
information you give them, really think about it, and
decide if that's the best course of action for them,"
she explained. For Srishti, success was seeing her
peers walk away knowing they had the power to be
heroes.

From Stage to Stethoscope

Reflecting on her journey, Srishti realized that the
project had fundamentally changed how she
viewed herself as a leader. She had gone from a
student who was nervous about middle school to a
young woman who could navigate statewide
partnerships and inspire a roomful of teenagers.
Beyond her work with organ donation, Srishti is a
girl of many artistic talents. She has been
practicing Indian classical dance, known as

Bharatanatyam, since she was five or six years old. This traditional dance helps her stay in touch with her culture and provides a stepping stone to her other creative passions, like playing the violin.

Srishti even uses her musical skills to give back, volunteering to play the violin for patients in the hospital. She realizes that even a five-minute piece of music can make someone just as happy as a massive community project could. "Even for two minutes helping someone, it still feels great," she noted. This desire to help led her to become a health equity high school ambassador, where she learned about the disparities marginalized communities face. She participated in activities that highlighted serious issues such as deportation fears and the denial of medical care, which deepened her interest in public health.

As she prepared for medical school, Srishti had a clear vision for her future. She aims to become a pediatrician or a mental health professional. Her advice to other girls considering taking on a massive project of their own is simple: "The more time and energy you put into your project, the more you're going to change as a person." She encouraged them to plan early so they could finish before the "craziness" of senior year began. Srishti has proven that, whether on a dance stage or in a medical clinic, she carries the heart of a leader.

Srishti's journey reminds us that life is like a beautifully woven tapestry, where every person's

story is a vital thread. By choosing to talk about the
things that others find difficult, she didn't just build a
project; she built a bridge of hope. Just as a small
seed can eventually grow into a forest that provides
life for many, Srishti's two-minute mission has
planted the seeds of awareness that will continue
to flourish, ensuring that the gift of life is never
again a silent or forgotten promise.

Chapter 13

Your Voice for Good

Tapestry of Transformation

As you have journeyed through these chapters, you have witnessed the incredible power of a young person's voice when it is fueled by purpose. You saw how a simple observation in a history class led to the preservation of an entire family's legacy through a digital archive that honors those held in incarceration camps. You read about the courage it took to stand before panels of adults and speak about the "silent word" of trauma, bridging an age gap that often keeps victims in the shadows. You followed the journey of a leader who turned a "taboo" subject like organ donation into a statewide challenge, proving that a two-minute choice can save up to eight lives. Each story served as a thread in a larger tapestry, showing that whether the mission involves building a "success closet" for women in need or mapping a county's local harvest, the heart of the work remains the same.

These stories also revealed the universal truth that leadership requires sacrifice and a refusal to settle for a "not as decent project". You learned that being "braver than you believe" often looks like staying home from prom to finish an advocacy documentary or facing repeated rejections from a council before your vision is finally understood. You saw leaders pivot during global pandemics, transforming local workshops into national virtual programs that reach girls from the Bay Area to across the United States. These narratives weren't just about the final awards; they were about the girls' internal growth—the shift from being "quiet and shy" to becoming vocal "hustlers" who know exactly who to ask for help. By witnessing their journeys, you have seen a professional roadmap for moving from a spark of innovation to a mission without end.

Igniting Your Own Flame

Now that you have heard the echoes of these healed voices and seen the digital voices given to the past, the question remains: what will you do with the fire you've found? The stories in this book were never meant to be just a collection of memories; they are a call to action for the leader residing within you. You are not a bystander in your community; you are a vital, life-saving source of information waiting to be released. Perhaps you have noticed a "deafening silence" in your own school, or maybe there is a "hidden history" in your neighborhood that only you have the curiosity to uncover. Whatever makes your heart "settle on change" is the very thing that should drive your next steps. Remember that you don't need a thousand-person audience to start; you only need the "grit" to begin and the passion to see it through.

The leadership transition happens the moment you decide that a problem is worth more than your comfort. It is about realizing that you are "smarter than you think" and capable of managing state-wide partnerships or international newsletters if you simply choose to try. As you move into the toolkit sections of this guide, think about the "big why" that will get you through the month-long lulls and the technical glitches. Choose a topic that makes you feel "carefree" and excited, because that love is the only thing that will make the "blood, sweat, and tears" feel like a joy. You are standing at a launchpad, ready to build your own bridge of hope. The following steps are the tools you need to build that bridge, ensuring that your voice becomes a permanent gift to the world.

A Guide To Using Your Voice

Using your voice for good requires a blend of passion, strategy, and technical skill. To help you navigate your own journey of change, we have created this toolkit based on the successful missions shared in this book. Every great project follows a specific set of operational steps that turn a vision into a reality.

Step 1: Identify the Gap. Look for the "silence" in your community or the "taboo" subjects that people prefer to ignore. Ask yourself what "settles in your heart" or makes you feel a sense of responsibility.

Step 2: Conduct Deep-Dive Research. Once you have your "why," find the "how". Dig into archives, search for primary source material, and look for the statistics that prove your cause is a real community crisis.

Step 3: Build Your Dream Team. You cannot do this alone. Reach out to experts like park rangers, school principals, or nonprofit directors. Choose a mentor who will keep you on track and push you when you're "swamped".

Step 4: Design the Blueprint. Create a curriculum or a structure for your work. Use professional tools—like high-end filming equipment, web design platforms, or graphic design software—to ensure your message is taken seriously.

Step 5: Make the Personal Connection. If emails aren't working, start making personal phone calls. People want to see your "personal connection with your project" before they decide to help.

Step 6: Handle the Logistics. Manage your budget by organizing fundraisers like bake sales or letter-writing campaigns. Be "resourceful" and find creative workarounds when your original plan is too expensive.

By following these steps, you can move beyond being a bystander and become a vital, life-saving source of information for your community.

Sustaining Your Movement

The final stage of using your voice for good is ensuring that your project outlasts your direct involvement. A true leader creates a "preserved time box" or a digital ecosystem that continues to provide value. This means you must focus on sustainability from the very beginning.

- **Create Permanent Resources.** Find a partner with a website to host your curriculum, videos, or maps so they are accessible to anyone with an internet connection.
- **Delegate and Partner.** Find an organization to manage the project after you move on, such as an Honor Society or a local ministry.
- **Document the Journey.** Be vigilant about capturing photos and videos of your process, as these digital tools are essential for sharing your story and proving your impact.
- **Stay Flexible.** Understand that things will rarely go exactly according to plan. When you hit a "speed bump" like a sudden deadline or a

technical glitch, stay calm and adjust your strategy.
- **Share Your Blueprint.** Don't just finish your project; give it to the world. Share your tips, curriculum, and results with others so they can recreate your success in their own neighborhoods.

Throughout this process, remember that the "more time and energy you put into your project, the more you're going to change as a person". You will learn how to "hustle," how to communicate with people from different backgrounds, and how to turn doubt into a standing ovation. Even small changes can make shifts in the world when driven by truth and passion. Your voice is like a seed that can eventually grow into a forest, providing life and hope for many. By choosing to speak up for what matters, you are building a bridge of hope and ensuring that no one else feels alone in the shadows. Your mission is not about reaching a finish line; it is about building a launchpad for the next generation of leaders.

ABOUT THE AUTHOR

Sheryl M. Robinson is a podcaster, mentor, and speaker dedicated to helping teens and young adults discover their unique gifts, talents, and abilities, creating a path toward their dreams.

Sheryl holds a Master of Arts in Servant Leadership from Viterbo University and a Bachelor's in Accounting from Southern Illinois University – Carbondale. She has been a proud member of Girl Scouts for more than 30 years. Her passion for supporting teens — especially those pursuing the Girl Scout Gold Award — led her to create *Hearts of Gold*, a YouTube series and podcast featuring Gold Award Girl Scouts from across the world.

In recognition of her work elevating and supporting the Girl Scout Highest Awards, Sheryl has been honored with the GSUSA Thanks II Award, the organization's highest recognition for service.

Recognizing the need for younger Girl Scouts to have resources and role models as they pursue the Bronze Award and Silver Award, Sheryl created this middle-grade book series to share inspiring stories of leadership, courage, and community change.

She deeply believes that the Girl Scout Highest Awards not only make the world a better place but also transform the Girl Scouts who earn them — building lifelong changemakers, confident problem-solvers, and compassionate leaders.

ACKNOWLEDGMENTS

Creating this book has been a journey shaped by many remarkable people, and I am deeply grateful for each of you.

To **my mom, Jean**, who first started me in Girl Scouts many years ago and planted the seeds of everything that would follow.

To **my daughter, Nikki**, a Bronze, Silver, and Gold Award Girl Scout whose dedication inspires me every day. Watching you flourish through each phase of your life is one of my greatest joys.

To **my husband, Mark,** thank you for always supporting me and the many plates you quietly set beside me while I typed away. I thank God for bringing you into my life every day.

To **Annalise,** thank you for reading the first draft and sharing thoughtful feedback. Your insights helped shape this book and made it stronger.

To **all the Gold Award Girl Scouts** who have shared their stories on the Hearts of Gold podcast — thank you for trusting me with your journeys. Your courage, creativity, and leadership inspire thousands.

To the **Girl Scout leaders, volunteers, and parents** who support these incredible young women: your encouragement makes meaningful change possible.

To **Cassie**, who encouraged me to restart my Girl Scout journey when my daughter joined Girl Scouts.

A heartfelt thank you to **Stacie and Shannan**, who have listened to me talk about this book for years and never stopped encouraging me to make it happen.

To **Walter**, my podcast editor for the first nine years, and **Tommy**, my new editor — and to their entire family, especially **Greg**, whose podcasting challenge a decade ago helped set all of this into motion.

And finally, to **Elsie, Rob, Cliff, Daniel, and Jessica** — thank you for your inspiration, for keeping the process fun, for sharing your knowledge, and for helping Hearts of Gold continue to grow.

This project exists because of each of you.
Thank you for helping bring these stories to life.

To all the future Bronze, Silver, and Gold Award Girl Scouts and others inspired by this book – Be the change you want to see in the world, and remember <u>your</u> leadership matters.

MORE STORIES

Want to hear more inspiring stories from Gold Award Girl Scouts?

HeartsofGoldPodcast.com

You can watch or listen to new episodes every month.

Podcast:
https://bit.ly/3JT7x0w

YouTube:
https://bit.ly/3P5nns8

Instagram:
https://bit.ly/3JZ2JX8